ROBIN HOLGA

G000241344

PREHISTORIC
FLINT MINES

SHIRE ARCHAEOLOGY

Cover photograph
A view of a typical gallery at Grimes Graves, Norfolk.
(Reproduced by courtesy of the Trustees of the British Museum.)

British Library Cataloguing in Publication Data:
Holgate, Robin.
Prehistoric flint mines.
I. Title.
553.65.
ISBN 0-7478-0141-X

Published by
SHIRE PUBLICATIONS LTD
Cromwell House, Church Street, Princes Risborough,
Buckinghamshire HP17 9AJ, UK.

Series Editor: James Dyer.

ISBN 0 7478 0141 X

First published 1991.

Printed in Great Britain by
C. I. Thomas & Sons (Haverfordwest) Ltd,
Press Buildings, Merlins Bridge, Haverfordwest, Dyfed SA61 1XF.

Contents

List of illustrations

All uncalibrated radiocarbon dates are signified by a lower-case bc.

Acknowledgements

I wish to thank all those who supplied illustrative material: Christina Unwin for the series of flint-mining drawings; Roger Mercer for the Grimes Graves shaft and Hambledon Hill photographs; the Sussex Archaeological Society for the Blackpatch and Harrow Hill shaft excavation photographs; the Trustees of the British Museum for the Grimes Graves gallery (on the cover) and flint-working area photographs; Owen Bedwin for the Harrow Hill aerial photograph; and Chris Grabham for printing the remaining Sussex photographs. I am also extremely grateful to Barbara Green, Keeper of Archaeology with Norfolk Museums Service, for information on the Norfolk flint-mining sites, and to James Dyer for reading and commenting on a draft of the text.

1
Introduction

The working of flint is the oldest known human industry in Britain. Before the use of metal, flint was fashioned into a range of tools and weapons. A hard, glassy substance occurring throughout much of southern and eastern England, flint is readily available and can be worked easily into any desired shape or form. By chipping off slivers, known as flakes, using another stone or a piece of antler as a hammer, a piece of flint can be shaped into a robust implement such as an axe. Alternatively, most flakes chipped off a lump of flint have razor-sharp edges and can either be used as impromptu cutting tools or shaped further into elaborate knives, piercing tools, scraping tools, strike-a-lights or tips for arrows.

Britain, previously joined by a land bridge to the European mainland, became detached from the continent over eight thousand years ago. By this time Britain was occupied by small groups of hunter gatherers who moved around the thickly forested landscape in search of wild foods and other natural resources. They mainly camped along rivers and the coast, at the forest margin, where a variety of edible and other resources was available. They hunted forest animals, mainly aurochs, deer and pig, for both meat and hides, the latter being made into clothing, bags and covers for wooden-framed shelters. Flint tools and weapons, often hafted in wooden handles or shafts, were used for hunting and working hides, wood, bone and antler. The emphasis in working flint was on the production of light, but durable, tool kits that could easily be carried from one place to another.

Around six thousand years ago Britain's inhabitants began to cultivate cereal crops and herd domesticated cattle, sheep and pigs. The craft of making pottery and manufacturing polished stone axes from flint and fine-grained igneous rocks became widespread. People began to restrict their movements to one part of the landscape, creating a mosaic of forest clearings, managed woodland and other activity areas where resources could be obtained and processed. This period, when early farming communities became established in Britain, is referred to by archaeologists as the new stone age or neolithic period, lasting over 1500 years up to $c.2000$ bc when the use of metal was first introduced to Britain.

The switch from exploiting wild foods to managing specific areas of land was associated with other changes in lifestyle. In destroying natural habitats these early farmers, as today, relied on maintaining soil fertility, the changing seasons and the weather to ensure good crop yields and rich grazing land. Ways of marking out land, transferring land ownership and settling boundary disputes between neighbours also had to be devised. It was partly due to this that monuments were built, for example causewayed enclosures and long barrows, where ceremonies could be enacted in thanksgiving to the gods for the health of their animals and a successful harvest, and in retaining friendly relationships between neighbouring communities. Votive offerings could be made or gifts exchanged as part of these ceremonies. It is evident from the nature of deposits found, both at causewayed enclosures and at other neolithic sites, that flint and other stone axes, apart from being necessary to help clear woodland and to shape timbers for house construction, were treasured items used for votive offerings or in gift-giving transactions.

It was in the neolithic period that flint mines were in use. Today over twenty flint-mining sites are known, surviving as lunar-like clusters of shallow craters and mounds which, in areas that have escaped the plough, are now covered with grass (figure 1). The archaeological investigation

1. Aerial view of Harrow Hill in 1976. (Photograph: Owen Bedwin.)

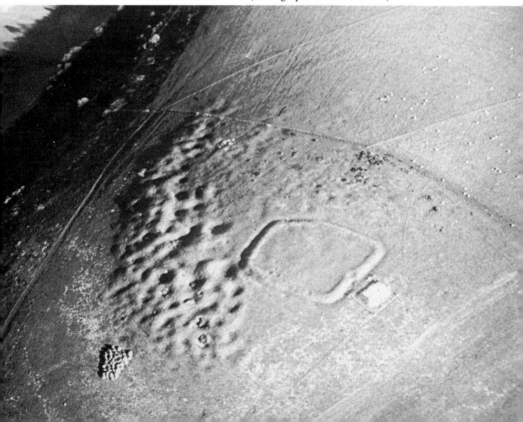

of these sites has shown that, although a wide range of tools and large cores was made and removed for use elsewhere, axes were the main implements being produced, especially at the South Downs sites. The existence of these flint-mining sites poses many questions. Where were they situated? When were they in operation? Who were the flint miners? How did they mine for flint? Why did they mine certain seams of flint and not others? What was the output and scale of production at these sites? And when and why were these sites abandoned? It is the purpose of this book to discuss these issues.

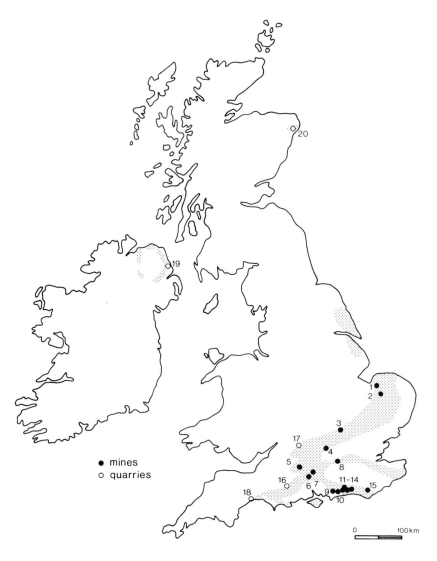

2. Map showing the location of known flint-mining sites in Britain: 1, Massingham; 2, Grimes Graves; 3, Pitstone Hill; 4, Peppard Common; 5, Durrington; 6, Easton Down; 7, Martin's Clump; 8, East Horsley; 9, West Stoke; 10, Long Down; 11, Harrow Hill; 12, Blackpatch; 13, Church Hill, Findon; 14, Cissbury; 15, Windover Hill; 16, Hambledon Hill; 17, Liddington; 18, Beer Head; 19, Ballygalley Hill (Ireland); 20, Buchan (Scotland). The stippling indicates the main areas of chalk with *in situ* flint. (Drawing: Robin Holgate.)

2
The distribution of sites

Flint mines have been found in most countries in northern Europe, stretching from Poland and Scandinavia to France and Britain. In Britain the distribution of the main flint-mining sites is restricted to the places where, as on the continent, undisturbed flint occurs in calcareous deposits (figure 2).

Flint was formed in layers or seams in the Upper Chalk, a sedimentary rock laid down over much of lowland Britain and Ireland during the Cretaceous period. Upper Chalk deposits with *in situ* flint seams occur today in southern and eastern England and in parts of Northern Ireland, where either solid bands of 'tabular' flint or layers of individual flint lumps called 'nodules' are encountered. Throughout Britain flint can be found in derived deposits, for example glacial drift, river gravels and beach deposits.

Flint nodules lying on the surface, apart from being relatively small in diameter, usually contain cracks and flaws resulting from frost action. The best flint for producing flint implements, in particular large implements such as axes, sickles and discoidal knives, was thus obtained by quarrying or mining into the Upper Chalk in order to reach unweathered flint seams. It is likely that a knowledge of where these seams occurred was acquired by examining surface exposures, for example coastal cliffs and under uprooted trees on valley slopes. It is also possible that clearing the land for cultivation and digging ditches associated with monuments helped expose seams and deposits from which flint could be extracted.

Flint mines are clustered, usually round the upper slope on one side of a hill, near where flint seams outcrop on the surface. The greatest concentration of flint-mining sites is on the South Downs in Sussex. Here the main group of four sites, Blackpatch, Harrow Hill, Cissbury and Church Hill, Findon, is situated on the highest hills on the block of downland between the rivers Arun and Adur. A second group of two sites, Long Down and West Stoke, lies on the southern edge of the Downs north of Chichester, whilst the other known group of flint mines, Windover Hill, is on the scarp slope of the Downs above the chalk-cut 'Long Man of Wilmington' figure. Interestingly, there are high-quality flint seams outcropping in parts of Sussex, for example on the downland scarp north of Brighton, which are not known to have been mined in the neolithic period. Elsewhere in Sussex, single shafts have been discovered at Slonk Hill, near Shoreham, and Nore Down, near West Marden.

The second concentration of sites is in Wessex. Two sites, Easton

Down and Martins Clump, occur on the Wiltshire-Hampshire border north-east of Salisbury; one lies at Durrington on Salisbury Plain in Wiltshire; and the remaining known site is situated at Hambledon Hill on the western edge of Cranborne Chase in Dorset. Another possible site, Liddington, is situated on the scarp slope of the Marlborough Downs in Wiltshire.

The most extensive flint-mining site in Britain is Grimes Graves, situated in the Norfolk Breckland. At Massingham, to the north of the Breckland on the west Norfolk chalk ridge, lies a second site. Reference has been made in the past to other possible sites in Norfolk, the most convincing of which are represented by the discovery of galleries following the line of flint seams exposed during ground disturbance at both Lynford and Westwick Street/Coslany Street, Norwich. Two red-deer antlers were found in the gallery at the latter site. Elsewhere in southern and eastern England, Peppard Common on the Chilterns and East Horsley on the North Downs are flint-mining sites of neolithic date sampled by excavation. On the Chilterns another probable site occurs at Pitstone Hill, on the scarp near Whipsnade, while a single shaft was discovered at High Wycombe and a possible group of mines has been identified at Whipsnade Zoo.

Outlying sites to this largely south-eastern distribution occur at Beer Head in Devon, Buchan in Aberdeen, Scotland, and Ballygalley Hill, County Antrim in Northern Ireland. Another possible site occurs at Flamborough Head, Humberside. These outlying sites are, strictly, quarry sites; deep flint mines are restricted to the Sussex, Norfolk and Wessex sites, where the best continuous seams of flint are to be found.

3
Mining for flint

Flint was extracted in one of two main ways. Where it was close to the surface, it could be quarried by digging shallow pits or working horizontally in the direction of the flint. In places where seams of flint were situated some way below the surface deep mineshafts were sunk.

The mining process

Flint outcropping at the surface could be extracted by open-cast and drift mining. There are two ways in which this could be undertaken. Chalk could be quarried horizontally, following a flint seam exposed at the surface until a vertical working face was created. From this face tunnels, or 'galleries', large enough for one person to crawl along were dug in further pursuit of the flint seam (figure 3). The maximum length of these galleries is about 2 metres, the approximate limit beyond which it became too dark and unsafe to work without artificial light and some form of gallery support. Alternatively, as practised on the western edge of Grimes Graves, open-cast mining was undertaken by digging small pits in honeycomb fashion over the area where the main flint seam on the site reached the surface.

Most galleries and pits were backfilled fairly rapidly after they were created. This has preserved both marks on the walls resulting from their original excavation and tools that were abandoned after use. The main mining tool used was a pick made from red-deer antler (figures 4 and 5). Most picks are made from shed antlers, which would have been gathered in late winter. All the tines except the brow tine were trimmed off using a flint knife. The pick would then be used to prize out the chalk, which has a fissured structure enabling it to be quarried in this way. At Grimes Graves perforated bone points, made from ox leg-bones, were found in the shallow pit fills on the north-western part of the site (figure 4). These were mounted on the brow tines of antler picks whose points had previously been worn or broken off. Marks on the chalk walls of some of the galleries at Grimes Graves show that stone or flint axes, mounted in wooden handles, were also used. The chalk rubble loosened by picks or axes was then scooped up into leather bags or baskets either by hand or by using an ox shoulder-blade shovel and antler rake (as was the case in Sussex: figures 4 and 6); wooden shovels may have been used as well.

In the areas where the flint seams were over a metre below the surface vertical shafts were dug. Most shafts were between 4 and 8 metres wide and up to 14 metres deep. These shafts were generally dug through two

3. A gallery from the open-cast mining area at Harrow Hill, 1986: (above) before excavation; (below) after excavation. (Photographs: Robin Holgate.)

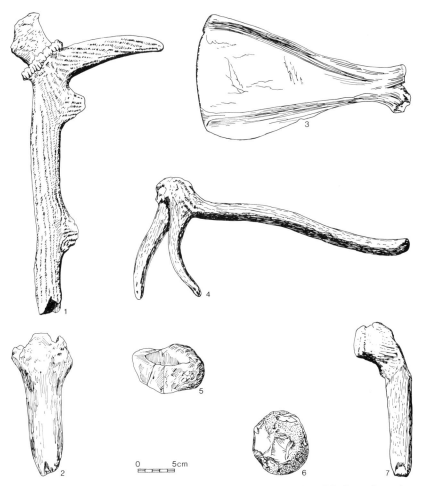

4. Flint-mining and flint-working implements: 1, red-deer antler pick; 2, perforated ox leg-bone point; 3, ox shoulder-blade shovel; 4, red-deer antler rake; 5, chalk cup; 6, flint hammerstone; 7, antler hammer. 1, 2, 5 and 6 are from Grimes Graves; 3, 4 and 7 are from Harrow Hill. (Drawing: Robin Holgate.)

or more layers of nodular flint before reaching the preferred flint seam just above floor level. At Grimes Graves the uppermost nodular flint layers are known as 'topstone' and 'wallstone', whilst the seam which was mined at the bottom of the shafts is known as 'floorstone' (figure 7). This seam was extracted by cutting down to the base and then levering up the flint in blocks. Galleries were then dug, radiating in all

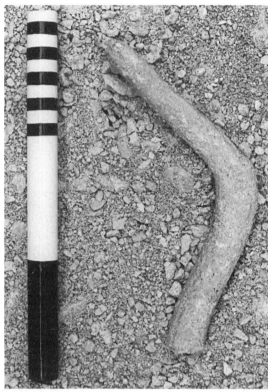

5. (Left) Antler pick fragment from Long Down, 1985. (Photograph: Robin Holgate.)

6. (Below) Ox shoulder-blade shovel from Long Down, 1985. (Photograph: Robin Holgate.)

7. A gallery at the floor of the shaft at Grimes Graves excavated in 1971, showing the remnant floorstone that was being mined. (Photograph: Roger Mercer.)

directions from the shaft at the level of the flint seam. These galleries were up to about 3 metres in length, joining up in some instances with galleries from neighbouring shafts.

Chalk rubble and blocks of flint could have been removed from the shafts in various ways. Archaeologists excavating flint mines since 1914 have hauled baskets or buckets of chalk rubble up by rope and pulley suspended from a wooden tripod erected over the entrance to the shafts. It is considered probable, though, that chalk waste was carried in baskets or leather bags up a wooden ladder (figure 8). One of the flint mines excavated at Church Hill, Findon, produced evidence for a wooden ladder, whilst excavations at Grimes Graves in 1971 discovered postholes associated with a probable platform a quarter of the way up the shaft. This could have been used as a stage for a ladder system to carry material out of the shaft and would also have served as a means of protecting miners working beneath from falling debris.

The chalk from each mine was either piled up around the lip of the mine or dumped in an abandoned mineshaft. The unweathered walls on

8. A typical flint-mining site in operation. (Drawing: Christina Unwin.)

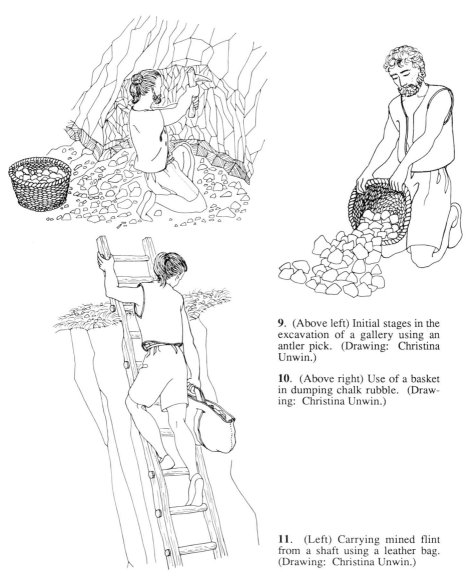

9. (Above left) Initial stages in the excavation of a gallery using an antler pick. (Drawing: Christina Unwin.)

10. (Above right) Use of a basket in dumping chalk rubble. (Drawing: Christina Unwin.)

11. (Left) Carrying mined flint from a shaft using a leather bag. (Drawing: Christina Unwin.)

most shafts suggest that they were backfilled fairly rapidly after they had been dug. It is likely, then, that as a new shaft was opened up old shafts were used as receptacles in which to dump soil, both to fill up a dangerous hole and to avoid heaping up spoil on ground required to sink adjacent shafts. Similarly, loose chalk quarried from a gallery was used to backfill recently excavated galleries in order to avoid the unnecessary removal of spoil from the shaft.

12. Producing axe roughouts at a flint-working area using an antler hammer. (Drawing: Christina Unwin.)

Mining was largely carried out using natural light. Carved chalk cups have been found which could have been filled with animal fat and used as lamps when working in dark recesses (figure 4). There is no evidence for the use of pit props and ceiling rafters to support the roofs of galleries. Careful examination at Grimes Graves showed that flint mines were designed with a series of narrow galleries and load-bearing walls, as opposed to straight galleries extending for some distance from the shaft. Thus a series of large shafts close together with numerous short galleries between them is not only a relatively safe system to operate without roof supports, but also an efficient and effective way of extracting a large percentage of the flint seam in the immediate vicinity of the shafts.

Working flint

The flint obtained by mining, once it had been brought to the surface, was initially dressed near the mine. This process mainly involved trimming off any irregular lumps with a spherical flint hammerstone (figure 4). The roughly shaped blocks of flint were then taken to an area where they could be worked into cores (carefully prepared blocks of flint from which flakes can be detached and then shaped into tools), axes and other implements (figures 13 and 14). These flint-working

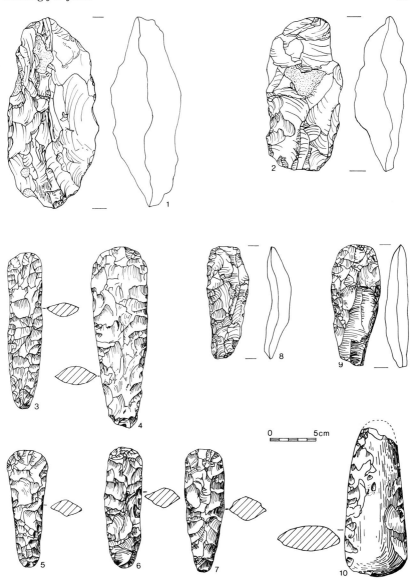

13. Flint implements from flint-mining sites: 1, axe roughout from Harrow Hill; 2, axe roughout from Long Down; 3 and 4, axe preforms from Church Hill, Findon; 5, axe preform from Cissbury; 6 and 7, axe preforms from Blackpatch; 8, axe preform produced on a flake from Long Down; 9, axe preform produced on a flake from Grimes Graves; 10, polished flint axe from Cissbury. (Drawing: Robin Holgate.)

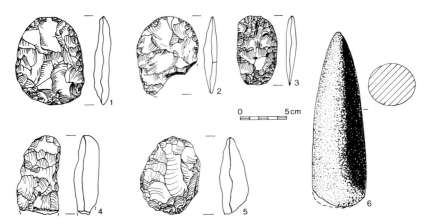

14. Flint and stone implements from flint-mining sites: 1, 2 and 3, discoidal knives from Grimes Graves; 4, sickle roughout fragment from Long Down; 5, discoidal knife from Long Down; 6, polished greenstone axe from Canon Greenwell's pit at Grimes Graves. (Drawing: Robin Holgate.)

areas were sometimes situated close to the mines themselves, as at Grimes Graves and Easton Down, and sometimes located on the edge of the mining area, as appears to have been the case at Harrow Hill and Long Down (figures 15 and 16). The remains of these working areas usually consist of a thick layer of flint flakes, shattered pieces of flint and fragments of axes and other implements which broke in the course of manufacture.

In the neolithic period axes were finished off by being ground and polished on a block of coarse-grained stone, for example sandstone or quartzite, using sand and water as a lubricant. There is no evidence, though, for the grinding and polishing of axes taking place at flint-mining sites. It is thus likely that implements which required finishing other than by flaking using hammerstones were prepared as roughouts and taken off site for further treatment. Most of these roughouts appear to have been flaked symmetrically at the flint-mining sites into forms, known as preforms (figure 13), that required only grinding and polishing to produce the finished artefact.

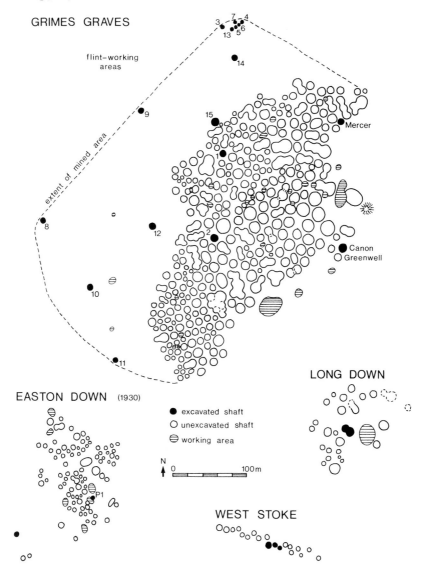

15. Plans of flint-mining sites in Norfolk, Wiltshire and West Sussex. (Drawing: Robin Holgate.)

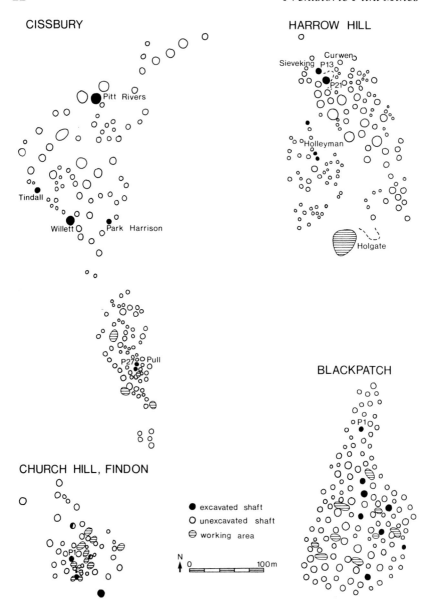

16. Plans of flint-mining sites in West Sussex. (Drawing: Robin Holgate.)

4
History of research

Early work

The flint mines at Grimes Graves and Cissbury were amongst the earliest archaeological sites to be excavated in Britain. Superficial work in 1852 by the Reverend S. T. Pettigrew and in 1866 by the Reverend C. R. Manning at Grimes Graves, and in 1857 by G. V. Irving at Cissbury, examined the upper fills of some of the mineshafts at these sites. Meanwhile, in 1859 C. B. Plowright investigated a group of pits, the deepest of which was nearly 8 metres deep, at Massingham, to the north of Grimes Graves. However, these early antiquarians failed to appreciate the full extent of these sites, with Irving concluding that the mines were cattle enclosures!

In the late 1860s further excavations took place at both Grimes Graves and Cissbury, resulting in the correct interpretation of these sites as flint mines. In 1867-8 General Pitt Rivers, then known as Colonel Lane Fox, and Canon Greenwell dug into about thirty pits at Cissbury. Although excavating only to a metre's depth, they discovered large numbers of flint flakes and thus inferred that the pits had been dug to extract flint for making implements.

The first full-scale investigation of a flint mine then followed in 1868-70 at Grimes Graves. Canon Greenwell, assisted in 1870 by Lord Rosehill, excavated one of the mines on the eastern side of the site. The floor of the shaft was 12 metres below the surface with galleries radiating in all directions. In addition to worked flints, the excavations produced antler picks, chalk cups, some enigmatic chalk carvings, animal bones and a polished greenstone axe (figure 14). Marks on the chalk walls of one of the galleries showed that this type of axe had been used during mining. Greenwell concluded that the mines at Grimes Graves dated to the neolithic period, largely on account of the domesticated animal bones found in the fill of the shaft.

Following Canon Greenwell's discoveries at Grimes Graves, in 1873-4 Ernest H. Willett and Plumpton Tindall each excavated completely one of the Cissbury shafts, thus determining their true depth. Tindall's shaft was over 12 metres deep, whilst Willett's was 6.5 metres deep. Pitt Rivers returned to the site in 1875 and investigated a further nine shafts. The fill of one shaft produced part of a pottery bowl (figure 17). In another shaft, over one of the gallery entrances, were a number of criss-cross markings in the chalk. But perhaps the most intriguing discovery was the skeleton of a young woman, buried head downwards near the bottom of a shaft. Either she had fallen in or her body had been

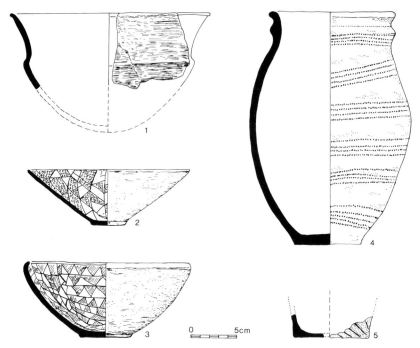

17. Neolithic and beaker pottery from flint-mining sites: 1, fragment of earlier neolithic carinated bowl from Cissbury; 2 and 3, fragmentary later neolithic Grooved Ware bowls from Grimes Graves; 4, beaker vessel from Church Hill, Findon; 5, fragment of later neolithic Grooved Ware vessel from Church Hill, Findon. (Drawing: Robin Holgate.)

placed head-first in what was an unusually narrow shaft, only 1.5 metres wide.

A colleague of Pitt Rivers, J. Park Harrison, continued working at Cissbury for the next two years, opening up the three mines immediately surrounding Willett's shaft and exploring the gallery system interconnecting them (figure 18). He also discovered a human skeleton, but this time that of a young man buried halfway down the shaft, lying on his side in a crouched position and surrounded by a single row of chalk blocks.

Further work and controversy

After the decade in the late nineteenth century of excavating shafts at Cissbury and Grimes Graves there was a lull of over thirty years before flint mines received further attention. In 1910-13 Major A. G. Wade

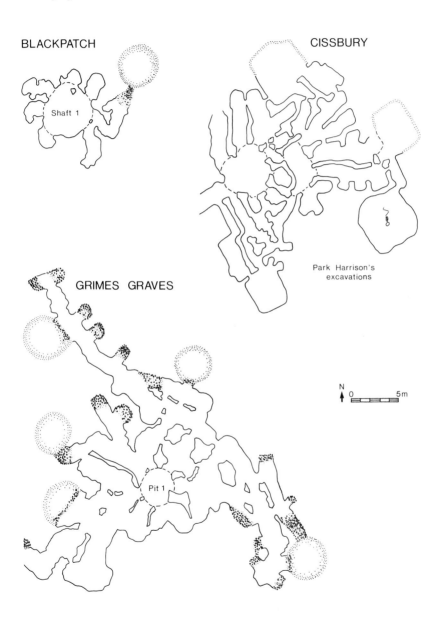

18. Plans of three excavated flint mines. (Drawing: Robin Holgate.)

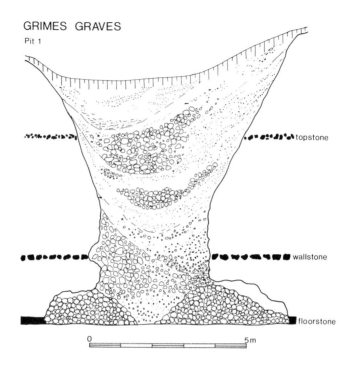

GRIMES GRAVES
Pit 1

topstone

wallstone

floorstone

0   5 m

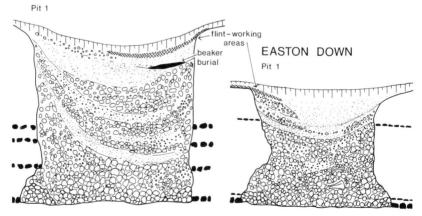

CHURCH HILL, FINDON
Pit 1

flint – working
areas

beaker
burial

EASTON DOWN
Pit 1

19. Sections of three excavated flint mines. (Drawing: Robin Holgate.)

excavated three of the shafts at West Stoke, recovering, amongst other material, a saddle quernstone. The shafts were 3 to 5 metres deep and, whilst no galleries were found, two of the shafts were undercut at the base, giving them a boot-shaped profile. On the Chilterns in 1912-13 Dr A. E. Peake excavated two shallow shafts at Peppard Common. In 1913 Reginald A. Smith reopened the first shaft and found it to be an open-cast pit. There were no signs of galleries in the sides of the pit.

Although Canon Greenwell's excavations at Grimes Graves had provided evidence that the site dated to the neolithic period, this apparent fact was refuted by Reginald Smith in 1912. Smith, Keeper of British and Medieval Antiquities at the British Museum, delivered a paper before the Society of Antiquaries of London, subsequently published in *Archaeologia* for that year, in which he suggested an old stone age or palaeolithic date for the mines. The large numbers of rough-shaped core tools from Grimes Graves were likened by Smith to palaeolithic implements, whilst the presence of domesticated animal bone was not considered as evidence for a neolithic date. Ingeniously, the greenstone axe found in one of the galleries excavated by Greenwell was equated with similar axes found in southern Scandinavia on shell midden sites which were then interpreted as pre-neolithic in date; since then, however, these sites have been dated to the fourth millennium bc.

Smith's paper was received favourably and his arguments for dating flint mines to the palaeolithic period became accepted. Largely stimulated by this controversy, Dr A. E. Peake began a further campaign of excavations at Grimes Graves.

Peake excavated two shafts in 1914 (figure 15, pits 1 and 2). Both shafts were about 9.5 metres deep and had galleries (figures 18 and 19). The filling of the shafts and galleries produced flint-mining tools, flint-working debris and neolithic pottery fragments. Also investigated in 1914 was a series of surface 'floors' or flint-working areas. In all, fourteen working areas were excavated, which Peake classified into two types: areas containing massive chipped pieces; and 'finishing floors' with both massive pieces and minute flakes.

The outbreak of war in August 1914 halted further excavation work but Peake's report, published in 1915, seems to favour a neolithic date for the flint mines. However, the report on the flintwork, written by Reginald Smith, assigns a palaeolithic date to the flints.

In 1916 Peake excavated twelve more flint-working areas, recovering a second greenstone axe from one of them. In 1917 he returned again to the site and began the excavation of three small pits on the north-eastern edge of the site; these were later termed 'primitive pits' by A. Leslie Armstrong.

Between the wars

Following Peake's work, a nineteen-year programme of excavations was started in 1920 at Grimes Graves under the direction of Armstrong. At first he excavated a further flint-working area where, in addition to flint-working debris, he recovered pieces of mined flint with engravings of red deer on the cortex and neolithic pottery fragments. He also dug a series of trenches over the whole site and demonstrated that, in some areas, the floorstone was as little as 150 mm below the ground surface. This suggests that the site could have initially been located relatively easily, and probably accidentally, by the prehistoric miners.

Over the next four years Armstrong excavated totally the three small pits opened by Peake in 1917, along with two further pits. These pits, situated on the valley side to the north-east of the visible mines, were up to 3 metres deep and without galleries. This led Armstrong to describe them as 'primitive pits' and infer that they represented the earliest phase of mining on the site. Furthermore, a mineshaft excavated in 1922 to the south of the primitive pits appeared to have rudimentary galleries at its base. Armstrong considered this shaft to be an example of an 'intermediate' group of pits, which were worked at a period between the primitive pits and the fully developed workings situated immediately to the south. This three-phase chronology, with the primitive pits assigned to the upper palaeolithic period, the intermediate pits to the middle stone age or mesolithic period and the fully developed pits to the early neolithic period, was elaborated upon in Armstrong's presidential address to the Prehistoric Society of East Anglia in 1926 and published in that year's *Proceedings*.

The final published excavation programme undertaken by Armstrong at Grimes Graves began in 1928 and continued in 1930 and 1932-3. This involved excavating five pits of the intermediate phase, with the excavation results being published in 1934.

After being demobbed in 1919 John H. Pull, a young postman from Worthing who had developed a strong interest in archaeology and geology in his childhood, discovered the group of flint mines at Blackpatch. In 1922-32 he investigated seven shafts and four working areas, along with twelve bronze age round barrows which overlie the site. The first shaft, excavated with help from the Worthing Archaeological Society, was over 3 metres deep with seven short galleries at its base (figures 18 and 20). One of the bronze age burials, a cremation accompanied by beaker pottery, was found underneath one of the flint-working areas, showing that flint on the site continued to be worked into the early bronze age. In 1932 Pull published these results privately in a book entitled *The Flint Miners of Blackpatch*.

Following Pull's work at Blackpatch the Worthing Archaeological

20. Excavation of shaft 1 at Blackpatch, 1922. (Photograph: Sussex Archaeological Society.)

Society, under the direction of Dr E. Cecil Curwen, excavated one of the flint mines on Harrow Hill. Curwen and his father, Dr Eliot Curwen, had helped Pull excavate the first shaft at Blackpatch in 1922. During this year Eliot Curwen recorded the Harrow Hill flint-mining site, situated on the hill immediately west of Blackpatch. Father and son, both general practitioners, had developed a passion for prehistoric archaeology and resolved to investigate the different classes of monument to be found on the South Downs. In 1924 Cecil Curwen selected one of the shafts on the northern edge of Harrow Hill for excavation (figure 21). It was 7 metres deep and some of the galleries on the north side of the shaft were interlinked with open-cast mining of flint seams at the point where they outcropped on the side of the hill. They recovered a variety of antler and bone tools, including picks, rakes and ox shoulder-blade shovels (figure 4). In 1936 the Worthing Archaeological Society returned to Harrow Hill where, under the direction of George Holleyman, they excavated a further three shafts on the summit of the hill.

In 1929 Dr J. F. S. Stone, whilst undertaking survey work on Salisbury Plain near the Wiltshire-Hampshire border, discovered a cluster of flint mines adjacent to an early bronze age settlement on Easton Down. Three years later he discovered a second flint-mining site, 3 km to the north-east on the same downland ridge at Martin's Clump, Hampshire. In 1930-4 Stone excavated six shafts and six flint-working areas at Easton Down, recovering flint-working debris, antler picks and neolithic pottery fragments. The shafts were 3 to 4 metres deep and, whilst the base of these shafts was undercut to extract flint, there were no galleries (figure 19). This was likely to be due to the weak nature of the chalk, which would have made the creation of galleries a hazardous task.

Whilst Armstrong was still a keen exponent of a palaeolithic date for the first phase of 'primitive' mining at Grimes Graves, the work at Easton Down prompted a fresh appraisal of the age of the British flint mines. In a paper of this title, published in the journal *Antiquity* for 1933, Grahame Clark and Stuart Piggott reviewed the accumulated evidence of sixty years' excavation work.

Clark and Piggott first met as schoolboys digging for Cecil Curwen in 1928 at The Trundle neolithic causewayed enclosure in West Sussex: later, Clark became Disney Professor of Archaeology at Cambridge University and Piggott became Abercromby Professor of Prehistoric Archaeology at Edinburgh University. In their article they described the location and nature of flint-mining sites in Britain and north-west Europe, discussed the pottery from Cissbury and Grimes Graves and ended with a critique of Armstrong's three-phase pit-digging sequence at Grimes Graves. They demonstrated that the stratigraphic association of neolithic pottery in Peake's 1914 shafts and Armstrong's 1920 flint-working area at Grimes Graves gave clear evidence for a neolithic date for all three of Armstrong's mining 'phases'. Furthermore, excavations at West Stoke and Easton Down, in addition to those at Grimes Graves, suggested that the different forms of pit reflected safety in working and economy in extracting flint. Clark and Piggott thus concluded that all the evidence pointed to a neolithic date for prehistoric flint-mining sites in Britain.

The article by Clark and Piggott was published before Armstrong produced his final publication on his 1928-33 excavations at Grimes Graves. Nevertheless, Armstrong criticised the article and continued to excavate three further shafts up to the outbreak of the Second World War, although he never reported on his final seasons' work. The last shaft that he worked on in 1939, on the north-west part of the site, is well known for the 'votive offering' discovered at the entrance to one of the galleries. This consisted of a pile of flint covered by antler and associated with a carved chalk female figurine, a chalk phallus and

21. Excavation of a gallery at Harrow Hill shaft 21, 1924. (Photograph: Sussex Archaeological Society.)

chalk balls. Although unproven, it is likely that this was a practical joke played on an unsuspecting Armstrong by one of his workers!

After Blackpatch, the results of which Clark and Piggott had harshly judged as unscientific and unreliable following a personal disagreement between John Pull and Cecil Curwen, Pull turned his attention to Church Hill, Findon. The site, situated on the next hill to the east of Blackpatch, was first surveyed by Herbert S. Toms in the early 1920s. Toms, the curator at Brighton Museum, had been employed by General Pitt Rivers as archaeological surveyor when he excavated sites on Cranborne Chase,

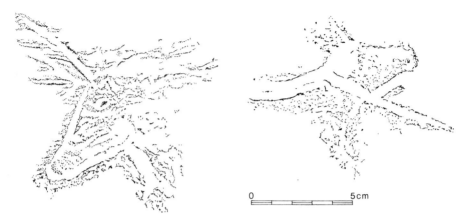

22. Animal head engravings from a gallery at Cissbury shaft 27, 1952-5 (after Pye). (Drawing: Robin Holgate.)

Dorset, in the late nineteenth century. In addition to recording Church Hill, he also carried out a fresh survey of Cissbury, the flint-mining site on the hill immediately east of Church Hill.

The Second World War and after

In 1933-52, with a break during the Second World War, Pull excavated six shafts, eight flint-working areas and eight bronze age round barrows at Church Hill. A series of pictograms had been cut into the roof of certain galleries in one of the shafts, whilst the upper fill of shaft 1 (figure 19) produced later neolithic Grooved Ware pottery and a human cremation burial in a beaker vessel (figure 17), overlain by a flint-working area.

In 1952-5 Pull transferred his operations to the flint mines on the south-western side of Cissbury, excavating three shafts and three flint-working areas. A skeleton of a young woman buried on her side in a crouched position was found on the floor at the entrance to one of the galleries in shaft 27, and three carvings of the heads of red deer and a short-horned bull were recorded on one of the gallery walls (figure 22). Towards the end of his life, Pull worked as a security guard and was fatally shot in a bank raid in 1961, before he could publish the results of his excavations at Church Hill and Cissbury.

After Cissbury one of Pull's assistants, E. F. Salisbury, spent two seasons in 1956 and 1958 excavating part of a shaft and two flint-working areas at Long Down, a small group of flint mines east of the site at West Stoke.

In Wessex a third group of flint mines was discovered in 1952 at Durrington in the side of a pipe trench. The site, investigated by A. St J. Booth and J. F. S. Stone, consisted of three open-cast workings and two shallow shafts with undercut bases. In Sussex a cluster of surface depressions at Windover Hill was excavated by E. W. Holden in 1953, confirming that the site was a small group of neolithic flint mines. On the North Downs the only known neolithic flint-mining site is at East Horsley, Surrey. In 1949 excavations by E. S. Wood showed that a shaft and two flint-working areas on the site were neolithic in date.

In 1957 A. E. P. Collins, whilst excavating a late prehistoric enclosure, found an open-cast mining site associated with a flint-working area and earlier neolithic pottery at Ballygalley Hill, County Antrim. This is the only flint-mining site so far known from Ireland.

Subterranean flint mines are unknown in Scotland. However, gravel deposits composed predominantly of flint occur in the Buchan area, near the coast north of Aberdeen. Over three hundred shallow 'flint pits' are known in one associated patch at Boddam Den, but none of these pits has been excavated to determine its nature and age.

The development and application of the radiocarbon dating technique in the late 1950s and 1960s was to revolutionise the study of prehistory. For the first time absolute dates could be assigned to organic material with confidence, thus enabling prehistoric sites to be dated accurately. Piggott's classic textbook on *The Neolithic Cultures of the British Isles*, published in 1954 as the first radiocarbon dates on neolithic material were becoming available, dated the neolithic period from 2000 to 1500 BC, whereas radiocarbon dating has now extended the period from 3500 to 2000 bc.

In the early 1970s the British Museum Radiocarbon Laboratory carried out a programme of dating antler and charcoal from flint-mining sites preserved in the British Museum and other museum collections. The Sussex mines generally proved to be dated to 3300-2700 bc, whilst Grimes Graves was dated to 2300-1300 bc. A date of 2350 ± 150 bc (BM-190) was obtained on an antler pick from Easton Down.

Fieldwork in the 1970s and 1980s

The results of the British Museum radiocarbon dating programme suggested that the Sussex flint mines were the earliest in Britain, whilst Grimes Graves came into production after mining had ceased at the Sussex sites. Further investigations then followed at both Grimes Graves and the Sussex sites to obtain more information on the nature, sequence and date of both the mining and the working of flint at these sites.

In 1971-2 Roger Mercer, an Inspector of Ancient Monuments with the Department of the Environment (which became the Historic Build-

23. Initial stages in the excavation of the shaft at Grimes Graves, 1971, showing the excavation method. (Photograph: Roger Mercer.)

ings and Monuments Commission for England in 1983), excavated one of the deepest shafts on the north-eastern side of Grimes Graves (figures 23 and 24), finding later neolithic Grooved Ware pottery on the floor of the shaft (figure 17). This was followed in 1972-6 by geophysical prospection and excavations by Gale de G. Sieveking on behalf of the British Museum. His work included the investigation of several open-cast pits 2 to 3 metres in depth on the north and west sides of the site, alongside which were numerous flint-working areas (figure 25); the re-excavation of Greenwell's shaft in 1974-6; and the investigation of two of the 'primitive pits', including the re-excavation of one of the pits excavated by Peake in 1917, on the north side of the site in 1976. In addition, he worked with P. J. Felder, a mining engineer from Maastricht in the Netherlands, to study the practicalities of flint mining in the neolithic period. At the same time Dr Mark H. Newcomer of the Institute of Archaeology, University of London, used flint from the site to carry out experiments in making axes and other implements in order to estimate the nature and scale of flint-working operations on the site.

In 1982 Sieveking began work at Harrow Hill on behalf of the British Museum, excavating the shaft immediately north-west of the one opened by Curwen in 1924-5. He also investigated the area in the vicinity of this shaft in 1984, in search of a flint-working area. Later that year the present author, as a Field Officer with the University College London Institute of Archaeology Field Unit, began a three-year project to assess damage by ploughing to the Sussex flint-mining sites. A flint-working area was located on the south side of Harrow Hill in 1984 and partially excavated in 1986, along with a series of open-cast pits. Further surveys and excavations of the flint-working areas at Long Down and Church Hill, Findon, were also undertaken in 1984-6 (figure 26).

24. Excavation of the floor of the shaft at Grimes Graves, 1971. (Photograph: Roger Mercer.)

Whilst excavations in the 1970s and 1980s focused on eliciting more information from Grimes Graves and sites in Sussex, Roger Mercer's work at the earlier neolithic causewayed enclosure complex at Hambledon Hill, Dorset, in 1981 uncovered an area of flint quarrying (figure 27). This previously unsuspected discovery draws attention to the scale and distribution of flint-mining sites in Britain. To date, sites leaving easily recognisable surface undulations have been identified as flint-mining sites, but how many small-scale sites leaving insignificant

26. Detail of the flint-working area at Long Down, 1985. (Photograph: Robin Holgate.)

surface indications remain to be discovered? Furthermore, the study of flint scatters brought to the surface of cultivated land by ploughing suggests the presence of a number of flint extraction and working sites on the chalk downs in southern England which otherwise leave no surface traces of mining activity. Clearly, there is still much work to be done to determine the complete range and location of flint-mining sites in Britain.

27. Flint quarries at Hambledon Hill, 1981. (Photograph: Roger Mercer.)

5
The sites

Archaeological fieldwork since the late nineteenth century has provided much information on the nature and scale of flint mining in the
neolithic period. Although some questions remain unanswered, there is
sufficient evidence of what was happening at the main flint-mining
sites to present a brief picture of each site.

Grimes Graves

The seam of superb quality flint known as floorstone occurs in south-
west Norfolk. At Grimes Graves over 360 shafts visible as surface
hollows and many more which are now completely filled and level on
the surface were dug to extract this flint seam. The site, occupying 37
hectares, consists of a tight cluster of deep mines on higher ground,
with a zone of open-cast mining to the north and west. The mines are 4
to 8 metres in diameter at the surface and up to 14 metres deep, with
galleries radiating from their bases. At the tops of shafts and in the
western and northern part of the site are scattered over one hundred
flint-working areas. At these working areas implements were manufactured from mined flint: the main products appear to have been axes,
some of which were produced on large flakes, and discoidal knives
(figures 13 and 14).

Neolithic pottery, notably Grooved Ware (figure 17), and discarded
antler picks have been recovered from the bottom of the deeper shafts.
Seventeen radiocarbon dates obtained from a selection of these picks
and charcoal range in date from 2320 ± 150 bc (BM-87) to 1340 ± 150
bc (BM-109). Five dates produced on antler and charcoal from the
shafts excavated by Canon Greenwell and Mercer range from 1865 ±
60 bc (BM-775) to 1814 ± 60 bc (BM-777).

Some of the earliest work on the use of land snails as indicators of the
past environment of archaeological sites was undertaken on samples
obtained from neolithic flint mines. In the early twentieth century A. S.
Kennard examined the snail shells from Grimes Graves, recording spe-
cies that favoured woodland habitats. Work by J. G. Evans on the snails
from the fill of the shaft excavated by Mercer suggests that when the
shaft was abandoned and partially infilled it was surrounded by woodland vegetation with dense leaf litter. It is likely that this woodland
cover spread over the entire site and beyond during the neolithic period.

Whilst excavating the upper fill of shafts on the southern and south-
eastern margins of Grimes Graves, domestic debris of middle bronze

age date was encountered. This included pottery, bronze and bone implements and large quantities of domesticated animal bones. Charcoal associated with this material has been radiocarbon-dated to 1134 ± 44 bc (BM-109). A farmstead was thus situated close to the southeastern edge of Grimes Graves at this time.

Blackpatch, Harrow Hill, Cissbury and Church Hill, Findon

The four highest hills on the South Downs north of Worthing are each crowned by flint-mining sites. Harrow Hill, the westernmost site, has about one hundred shafts visible, dug to exploit four seams of nodular flint outcropping on the hillside. Open-cast mining of the lowermost seams took place on the northern and southern edges of the site, and perhaps along the eastern edge as well. One substantial flint-working area has been investigated, where, amongst other implements, axe roughouts were being produced. Seven radiocarbon dates, averaging around 2900 bc, have been obtained on antler and charcoal. Analysis of the snail shells from the fills of the shaft excavated by Sieveking and the open-cast mines on the southern side of the hill shows that the site was surrounded by woodland in the neolithic period.

Blackpatch, immediately east of Harrow Hill, was bulldozed flat by the farmer in the 1950s. Pull recorded 64 shafts on the site. The shafts he excavated varied from 1 to 3 metres in depth, all exploiting a single seam of nodular flint. About ten flint-working areas were found interspersed amongst the mines, at least one of which dates to the early bronze age. Axe preforms and roughouts predominate amongst the implements recovered from the working areas. A single radiocarbon date of 3140 ± 150 bc (BM-290) has been obtained on an antler pick from one of the galleries excavated on the site.

To the east of Blackpatch is Church Hill, Findon, where Pull recorded 36 shafts. The shafts excavated by Pull were 3 to 6 metres deep, the deepest cutting through six nodular flint seams. The galleries radiated from the base of the other excavated shafts, mostly exploiting the fourth deepest flint seam. Fourteen flint-working areas in between the shafts were investigated by Pull, dating to the neolithic and early bronze age, where a range of implements including axes, chisels, miniature axes and discoidal knives was produced. An antler pick from one of the galleries produced a radiocarbon date of 3390 ± 150 (BM-181).

Cissbury, the site furthest to the east, consists of over one hundred shafts, the deepest of which is over 12 metres deep, cutting through six flint seams. Three flint-working areas have been excavated on the southern part of the site, with axe preforms and roughouts forming the largest proportion of the implements recovered. Three radiocarbon dates centring on 2750 bc have been produced on antler picks obtained from galleries excavated on the site.

Middle and late bronze age pottery was also recovered from the surface deposits at Harrow Hill and Church Hill, Findon, showing that
these sites were farmed from nearby settlements in the late second
millennium bc.

West Stoke, Long Down and Windover Hill

There are two sites on the southern edge of the South Downs north of
Chichester, both excavated to extract single seams of nodular flint. At
West Stoke a line of about twenty shafts without galleries was dug to a
depth of 3 to 5 metres. As yet, no flint-working areas have been found
here. To the east of West Stoke is Long Down. This site consists of
about twenty mines with at least one large flint-working area where
axes, some of which were made on large flakes, sickles and discoidal
knives were produced. Two radiocarbon dates around 3000 bc were
produced on an antler pick and an ox shoulder-blade from the upper fill
of a shaft partially excavated in 1985, whilst snail shells from the same
deposits suggest that the flint mines were surrounded by woodland at
the time when they were abandoned. Middle and late bronze age pottery was also found on the surface of the site, indicating the presence of
a nearby contemporary farmstead.

The other site of note in Sussex is Windover Hill, where a group of
about nine hollows and associated upcast dumps have been proved by
excavation to be neolithic flint mines.

Easton Down, Durrington and Hambledon Hill

There are about one hundred shafts at Easton Down dug to exploit the
one seam of nodular flint outcropping on the hill. At least seven flint-
working areas interspersed between the shafts have been recorded, where
axe and chisel preforms and roughouts predominate amongst the implements that were being produced. A single radiocarbon date of 2530 ±
150 bc (BM-190) was obtained from an antler pick excavated from
shaft 1.

Other flint-mining sites in Wessex that have been excavated include
Durrington and Hambledon Hill. At Durrington in Wiltshire three
open-cast pits and two shafts 1.5 metres deep were excavated to extract
a seam of poor-quality flint. The fill of one shaft produced a later
neolithic flint arrowhead. Hambledon Hill in Dorset consists of about
ten pits or quarries, also dug to extract a thin seam of poor-quality flint.
Galleries interlinked some of these pits, the fills of which produced
fragments of antler mining tools and earlier neolithic pottery. It is
likely that many more sites similar in nature to Durrington and
Hambledon Hill existed in Wessex during the neolithic period.

Peppard Common and Pitstone Hill

At Peppard Common, Oxfordshire, there are at least two small groups of flint mines. One group has been excavated and consists of two pits, 4 metres and just over 1 metre deep respectively, with a flint-working area in between. These pits were open-cast workings, the deeper of the two quarrying a horizontal layer of flint outcropping on the hillside for a distance of 12 metres. Discoidal knives, axe preforms and roughouts are the main implements recovered from the site.

At Pitstone Hill, Buckinghamshire, a small group of three possible flint mines associated with upcast dumps has been recorded, although the site has yet to be sampled by excavation.

East Horsley

Excavations at East Horsley in Surrey have revealed a mine 4 metres deep cutting through four flint seams and two flint-working areas dating to the neolithic period. A second shaft on the site, dating to the medieval period, had been used to extract flint for building a neighbouring house.

6
Flint mining and the neolithic period

The Sussex flint mines, where the flint was used largely for producing axes, were in operation during the late fourth and early third millennia bc. Flint continued to be worked into axes, discoidal knives and other implements at some of these sites until at least the end of the third millennium bc, but using nodules left on site as opposed to freshly mined flint. Grimes Graves and probably Peppard Common were in production in the late third and early second millennia bc and, whilst axes were manufactured, discoidal knives form a significant proportion of the roughed-out implements found at both sites. The Wessex sites were certainly active in the late third millennium bc, although it is possible that mining started at Easton Down around the same time as the Sussex mines were in operation.

Whilst large quantities of flint were extracted at the various mining sites in southern and eastern Britain, a study of flintwork from domestic and other neolithic sites shows that mined flint accounts for a very small proportion of the flint in general circulation. In most areas flint obtained from local beach, river gravel, drift, clay-with-flints or downland sources was exploited for making the range of cutting, scraping and piercing tools and weapons in everyday use. The flint-mining sites, then, appear to have served as sources of flint for specific purposes. It could be argued that mining was simply a means of extracting flint on a large scale in places where high-quality seams of flint happened to have been located. If this had been the case, it is surprising that mining did not take place in other localities where neolithic people knew of the existence of flint seams suitable for mining. Instances such as this, situated close to domestic sites, occurred in Sussex, for example along the scarp of the Downs north of Brighton. It is thus likely, particularly given the apparent emphasis on producing a limited range of tools, that flint-mining sites were specialist production centres.

Stone quarrying and axe production in Papua New Guinea

It is appropriate at this stage to consider how a twentieth-century simple farming society using stone technology quarried or mined stone for axe production. The Tungei tribe in Papua New Guinea, until metal tools were introduced in the 1930s, excavated thousands of tonnes of rock at each of a number of quarry sites to obtain stone for making axes. These axes were then traded over a 250 km radius from their sources. Their quarry sites consisted of a 2 km line of pits in the Papua New Guinea highlands. All the men in the seven quarry-owning clans of the

Tungei, upwards of two hundred men and adolescent youths, would go on quarrying expeditions at intervals of three to five years. The demand for axes ultimately led to the need for an expedition but social forces, stemming from the Tungei belief system, controlled the exact timing. The success in obtaining stone from the axe quarries depended on ritual purity and the correct axe-making magic. Spirits and the tribal ancestors were considered to control access to the axe stone, and pigs were sacrificed for them at the start of an expedition.

The quarrymen left their homesteads and moved to camps at each of the quarries, situated up to 5 to 7 km away from their homes, for the duration of the expedition. The drier months from May to November were the best time for an expedition. Quarries were surrounded by primary forest. No farming took place nearby and food was supplied daily by the quarrymen's wives. The end of an expedition was marked by a small celebratory pig kill and a ritual fight to drive away the spirits of the axe quarries. Finally the wives collected the axes in net bags and everyone returned to the settlements in the valley below.

There was no form of coercion from a strong central tribal leader to mobilise quarry workers: the desire to compete successfully with exchange partners drawn from various neighbouring tribes was a powerful incentive for individuals to go quarrying. Personal ambition had to be conceded to working co-operatively on the potentially dangerous work of quarrying, and this was partly achieved by ensuring equality in the final sharing out of axes.

All those taking part in the expedition would have ten to fifty roughouts for producing polished axes to dispose of in any way they wanted. A good number of these roughouts would be made into small work axes, up to 15 cm in length, while only a few would be of sufficient size (over 20 cm long) and quality for high-prestige transactions such as brideprice. No individual would produce more than a handful of polished axes in one year; most axes would have left Tungei territory as unpolished roughouts in order to meet commitments with exchange partners.

It has been estimated that between 40,000 and 300,000 axes per century were produced, a figure easily consumed by the population of about one million living in the trade hinterland of the highland provinces.

Mining for flint in Britain

Neolithic communities in Britain cannot be compared directly with the Tungei tribe. The description of Tungei quarrying expeditions does, however, give an example of the nature and scale of axe production that can be achieved by stone-using societies. The results of fieldwork, particularly in recent years, have gone some way towards elucidating the character of flint production at the British mining sites.

Analysis of the chalky rubble fill of flint mines has provided information on the environment and weather conditions prevailing at the time these sites were in operation. A study of the snail shells extracted from many of the Sussex flint mines and Grimes Graves shows that flint-mining sites were situated in small forest clearings at some distance from agricultural land. In addition, the sides of most mines are unweathered and there is little evidence for the accumulation of sediments that have been washed in by rainwater. This suggests that mining was a seasonal activity undertaken during the drier summer and early autumn months. Furthermore, Canon Greenwell's pit at Grimes Graves was abandoned before all the galleries had been exploited, indicating that mines could have been in operation for a limited period. Clearly, shafts and their network of galleries were not left open for flint to be extracted intermittently over a number of months; each mine was more or less fully excavated and at least partially backfilled before being abandoned.

There is no evidence for contemporary domestic activity at any of the flint-mining sites. The miners either travelled from where they lived to the mine each day or camped nearby for the period when mining took place. The results of fieldwork and analysis of flint collections in museums throughout much of southern and eastern Britain largely carried out in the 1980s show that the first farmers lived mainly on the chalk and limestone upland areas, for example the South Downs, Salisbury Plain and the Cotswolds. By the end of the neolithic period settlement was widespread, taking in most of the previously settled upland areas and also the major river valleys. The flint-mining sites, if not immediately alongside settlements, would therefore have been situated relatively close to the places where people lived at the time when they were in use.

The archaeological investigations by Mercer and Sieveking at Grimes Graves looked in detail at the nature of neolithic flint mining. It became apparent that a carefully planned system was pursued of excavating large shafts close together with narrow galleries and strategically positioned load-bearing walls. This reflects the high degree of ingenuity, skill and organisation of the miners who undertook this work.

Concerning the amount of work and length of time involved in flint mining, radiocarbon dating suggests that Grimes Graves and the Sussex sites were each worked over an average of three hundred years. If mines were opened at a constant rate, then no more than one or two shafts a year at the most would have been dug, implying that this would have been sufficient to supply the miners or their market with flint for one or two years. Following the excavations in the 1970s at Grimes Graves, it has been calculated that a team of up to twenty able-bodied workers could excavate and extract flint from a mine with radiating galleries in a minimum of two months. Fewer people, though, would have worked more efficiently and effectively in the confined space at the bottom of each shaft. Open-cast mining would have been a much smaller-scale operation, taking two or three people less than one or two days at the most to open up and exploit an open-air quarry. Given that shafts were not left open for long, and with the safety risks inherent in mining, it is probable that a specialist or experienced team of workers was responsible for excavating each shaft.

A team of flint miners would have to be fed and supported by the neolithic communities living in the area. One example of the resources needed for each mining operation is the use of antler tools. Discarded antler picks are encountered in the fill of most flint mines. The four shafts excavated by Canon Greenwell in 1868-70, Peake in 1914 and Mercer in 1971 at Grimes Graves yielded over 570 picks, most of which were made from shed antlers. It has been calculated that twenty to forty deer could supply the antlers for picks found in one shaft and, with an average of 100 to 150 picks per shaft, the total number of antlers represented at Grimes Graves as a whole would be 40,000 antlers from 24,000 male deer. Assuming that all antler was recovered and that all suitable antler was used, this would mean the existence or maintenance of a standing population of 120 deer to supply the miners excavating each shaft. Given this and the other resources needed to support a team of full-time workers, it is likely that, assuming mining was an annual event, no more than one team was released to excavate one or two shafts per site a year.

Scale of output

The work by Mercer and Sieveking at Grimes Graves generated estimates for both the time involved in excavating one shaft and the number of flint implements manufactured on site. Each galleried shaft produced about 40 tonnes of floorstone, giving a figure in excess of 14,000 tonnes for the entire site. If exploited to its full potential, this would enable in excess of fifty thousand implements per shaft to be produced, or around 25 to 30 million implements from the site as a whole.

Experiments to replicate axes carried out in the 1970s at Grimes Graves showed that it takes about ten to twenty minutes to produce the rough outline of an axe, generating up to four thousand flakes in the process. In addition, the experiments indicated that the scatter patterns of the flakes from the neolithic working areas resulted from the manufacture of numerous roughouts, rather than merely one or two. In some cases the position of the flint worker's 'seat' could be recognised by the occurrence of a blank area in the scatter pattern. It would thus have

been possible for one or two flint workers to produce substantial quantities of implements in a semi-finished form at the same time that flint
was being mined.

However, the large quantity of rough trimmings, shattered pieces and
flakes amongst the flintwork making up the working areas at Grimes
Graves shows that flint was not worked as economically as it could
have been. Furthermore, it is unknown whether or not flint was taken
from the site in any quantity for working elsewhere. This, in addition to
the fact that a range of implements was produced at Grimes Graves,
makes it difficult to estimate the number of axes, discoidal knives and
other implements manufactured there.

The market for mined flint

Axes were certainly one of the main products of the Sussex flint
mines. Examination under a microscope of the edge-wear patterns on
flint axes shows that some axes were used for felling trees and working
wood. Study of both the distribution of flint axes and the contexts from
which they have been recovered, though, suggests that some axes at
least were also put to other uses.

Both flint axes and axes made from fine-grained igneous rock are
found in varying densities throughout Britain, often occurring at con-
siderable distances away from their individual sources. This movement
could be the result of either direct trade or exchange. Although the
existence of entrepreneurs who created a network of markets for trading
axes is a possibility, the distribution patterns for axes from each known
geological source are compatible with a 'down-the-line' exchange system. Such a system not only involves the straightforward exchange of
one set of goods for another but also includes any transfer of material
objects that took place as a form of gift giving. The repeated hand to
hand exchange of the same items would gradually lead to their movement further away from their point of origin. Furthermore, tougher and
more hard-wearing axes would stay longer in circulation and thus travel
further from their sources. The distribution pattern produced by this
system, a gradual decline in numbers of axes with increasing distance
from source, is largely apparent for neolithic axes in Britain (figure 28).
In addition, brittle flint axes have much more restricted distributions
than the tougher axes made from fine-grained igneous rock. There are
instances, however, when high-density peaks of particular axes occur
some distance away from their place of origin, an example being the
unexpectedly high number of Cornish greenstone axes in East Anglia.
This could come about through a more complex form of exchange,
perhaps using redistribution centres in some areas away from the axe
source. Alternatively, certain axes might have been put to specific uses,

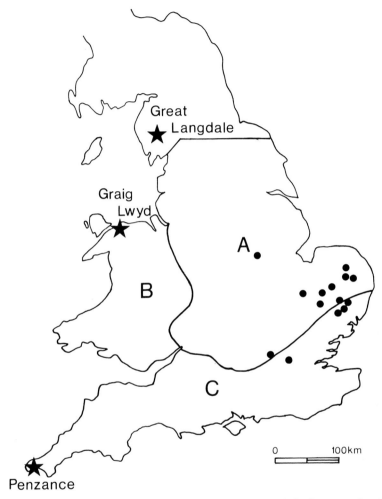

28. Dominant stone axe groups and the areas in which each is the most abundant individual group: A, area in which Great Langdale axes are dominant; B, area in which Graig Lwyd axes are dominant; C, area in which Cornish axes from near Penzance are dominant (after Cummins). Also illustrated is the distribution of eastern flint axes with, as yet, no precisely determined source (after Pitts). (Drawing: Robin Holgate.)

resulting in higher proportions of these axes occurring in some parts of Britain. It is thus necessary to look at the contexts in which axes have been found to see if this throws any light on the function of axes.

A study by Julie Gardiner in the 1980s of the distribution of flint axes in central southern England shows that most axes are found on the chalk downs, precisely the area where evidence for settlement is concentrated. Furthermore, whilst a large number of broken and reworked axes occur on the Downs, a larger proportion of polished axes recovered from the coastal plain south of the Downs and from the Weald to the north-east are complete and often in pristine condition. In the Thames basin, the large number of complete axes retrieved from the river Thames and other watery contexts is striking. In some cases hoards of over a dozen axes, including both preforms and polished axes, have been recovered. An example of a carefully excavated watery context where complete axes were found, showing that they result from deliberate deposition, is the Sweet Track in the Somerset Levels. This wooden catwalk structure, radiocarbon-dated to 3200 bc and running from the Quantock Hills to a sandy island across a peaty quagmire, had broken pottery bowls and stone objects placed at intervals along its length. Amongst the stone objects were a beautiful polished axe of jadeite, a stone imported from the European continent, and a flint axe preform. Both were unhafted and in pristine condition, undoubtedly positioned intentionally by the track. Clearly, these axes were not intended for mundane use in any way. In all probability they were seen as 'symbols of wealth', objects to be treasured and used in specific transactions, for example as votive offerings.

The role of flint mines
Gardiner's study of flint collections in museums in southern England has shown that at least half of the flint axes recovered from the Sussex Downs were made from locally obtainable surface flint. It was also shown that their distribution is related to that of domestic sites which are later in date than the Sussex flint mines. As some axes at least appear to have been wealth objects for use in various transactions, the mining of good-quality flint in Sussex might have developed to supply the market in these objects. The mining sites themselves were worked seasonally by local communities who realised that the good-quality flint for producing axes that they had access to was a valuable resource. The possession of this resource would have enabled the communities in Sussex and Wessex to generate objects that were highly sought after by neighbouring communities, thus enhancing their own wealth and status. The mines at Grimes Graves and Peppard Common might have been in operation for a similar reason, except that the emphasis in demand at the end of the late third millennium bc had switched from axes to discoidal knives.

Apart from industrial activity, rituals and ceremonial activities associated with life at the time also took place at flint-mining sites. The pottery vessels found at Cissbury and Grimes Graves (figure 17), along with the chalk carvings at Cissbury (figure 22) and Church Hill, Findon, and the human burials at Cissbury, are not the usual items expected to be associated with mining. The human burials were intentionally placed in the flint mines; they might have been individuals who died at the time when mining was taking place or, in the light of later prehistoric sacrificial victims preserved in peat bogs in northern Europe, could possibly have been sacrificed when the mine was being abandoned. Flint-mining sites, particularly the Sussex sites, were usually false-crested and might thus have been visible above the tree line as gleaming white mounds from a distance. In this respect, in addition to the human burials and the ceremonial deposits, they resemble a number of the causewayed enclosures and long barrows in existence at the same time. The flint mines can thus be seen as one of a series of short-term activity sites in seasonal use during the neolithic period, either annually or when there was the demand for further flint from these sites.

The end of neolithic flint mining

The demise of flint mining in Britain was due to changes in the relations of distribution as opposed to relations in production. The flint miners in southern and eastern England could, no doubt, have continued to mine flint and produce implements from it but without a means of receiving payment for this labour there would be no incentive to continue production. The end of mining at the Sussex sites coincides with changes in the use and construction of enclosures and barrows and the development of new styles of pottery and stone implements. There was also an increase in the number of, and area occupied by, domestic sites. Flint axes continued to be used on domestic sites, but there is evidence that a number of axes in use at this time were made from locally available surface flint. Thus social and economic changes probably led to a decline in the market for flint axes from mined flint.

Similarly, mining and implement production at Grimes Graves and any other sites still in use ceased at about the time that hard-edged metal tools were introduced to Britain. Whether or not it was the technological change from stone to bronze or other changes in economy and society that led to the abandonment of the last prehistoric flint-mining sites is unclear. What is apparent is that new wealth objects, for example bronze flat axes, were being produced at the time the early second millennium bc flint mines and their products went out of use.

Flint mining since the prehistoric period

Flint has been used for a variety of purposes since the prehistoric period. Throughout much of eastern and southern England flint is the most common naturally occurring stone suitable for building. First used during the Romano-British period, flint continued to be quarried, collected from beaches or picked up from the surface of cultivated fields for building work into the twentieth century. During the fifteenth century flint nodules were shaped into squares and fitted together in the same way as bricks to produce elaborate chequered designs known as flushwork.

From the seventeenth to the early eighteenth century flint was an ingredient in manufacturing glass. From the early eighteenth century up to today flint has been used for producing pottery. For both purposes flint has largely been collected from the pebble-strewn beaches of south-east England and Normandy.

In the early seventeenth century the flintlock gun was invented, using a flint to create a spark to fire the gun. By the mid eighteenth century there was a huge demand for gun-flints, leading to the quarrying and mining of flint for their production. Quarrying took place at a number of places, for example Clarendon, near Salisbury, in Wiltshire, Beer Head in Devon and on the Thames near Grays in Essex, but the place where mining and gun-flint production reached its zenith was Brandon in Suffolk, immediately south of Grimes Graves. Here, a large area of barren Breckland known as Lingheath became a flint-mining site, with shafts being sunk up to 14 metres deep in order to exploit the floorstone. The last miner, Arthur 'Pony' Ashley, was over eighty years of age when he finally stopped working in the late 1930s. Since then the gun-flint industry has finished, but some flint is still obtained on a small scale from chalk and gravel quarries in the Brandon area for use in the building trade today.

7
Sites to visit

Grimes Graves, six of the main flint-mining sites in Sussex and Pitstone Hill all survive as earthworks, although some of the Sussex sites have been partially flattened by ploughing in the 1970s and 1980s.

Church Hill, Findon, West Sussex (OS 198: TQ 114083). 4¹/₂ miles (7 km) north-west of Worthing.
 This site has largely been levelled by ploughing. It consists of about thirty flint mines, accessible by public footpath, on the south-east side of the hill, overlooking Cissbury.

Cissbury, West Sussex (OS 198: TQ 137078). 4 miles (6 km) north of Worthing.
 This site is the easiest and most spectacular of the Sussex sites to visit. The site is owned by the National Trust and visitor car parks are situated east of Findon. The summit of the hill is crowned by the ramparts of an iron age hillfort. The flint mines occur mainly within the western part of the hillfort but also continue under and outside the hillfort on the southern side of the hill. Over one hundred shafts are visible as depressions measuring up to 6 metres in diameter and 3 metres deep. On a clear day, the site offers good views of the surrounding downland landscape and the coastal plain around Worthing. Church Hill is also visible to the west behind Findon parish church.

Grimes Graves, Norfolk (OS 144: TL 820900). 6 miles (9.5 km) north-west of Thetford. Telephone (visitor centre): 0842 810656.
 This is the best known flint-mining site in Britain. The site is managed by English Heritage (the Historic Buildings and Monuments Commission for England) and a car park and visitor centre are provided at the site. Some 360 shafts can be seen as hollows, averaging 5 metres in diameter and 2 metres in depth. One of these shafts, the first pit excavated by Dr A. E. Peake in 1914, is open for visitors to go down and see seven galleries radiating from the bottom of the shaft. The visitor centre has displays with antler mining tools and worked flints which show how flint was mined and worked at the site in the neolithic period.

Harrow Hill, West Sussex (OS 197: TQ 082100). 5¹/₂ miles (9 km) north-west of Worthing.
 This is an impressive site accessible by public footpath. About one hundred flint mines cluster in an arc around the north-east side of the

hill, partly surrounding and underlying a small iron age hillfort near the summit. The mines are about 6 metres in diameter and 3 metres deep.

Long Down, West Sussex (OS 197: SU 932093). 5 miles (8 km) north-east of Chichester.

This site consists of a group of about twenty mines on the west side of Long Down, approachable by public footpath.

Pitstone Hill, Buckinghamshire (OS 165: SP 950140). 2 miles (3.5 km) north-west of Tring.

This site is a cluster of about three possible mines, accessible by public footpath, on the southern side of the hill.

West Stoke, West Sussex (OS 197: SU 832096). 3 miles (5 km) north-west of Chichester.

This site consists of a faint line of about twenty mines immediately north of Stoke Clump and can be reached by public footpath.

Windover Hill, East Sussex (OS 199: TQ 543033). 5 miles (8 km) north-west of Eastbourne.

This site is a cluster of about nine mines situated on the South Downs scarp above the Long Man of Wilmington chalk-cut figure. The site is accessible by public footpath and can also be viewed from Wilmington Priory, where there is an information board indicating the position of the mines in relation to the Long Man of Wilmington.

8
Museums

Much of the material excavated at Grimes Graves is in the British Museum, London, whilst Worthing Museum contains a significant proportion of the excavated material from Sussex. Comprehensive displays of mining equipment, flint-working tools and roughouts can be seen at the following museums:

Ancient House Museum, White Hart Street, Thetford, Norfolk. Telephone: 0842 752599.

Ashmolean Museum of Art and Archaeology, Beaumont Street, Oxford OX1 2LM. Telephone: 0865 278000.

British Museum, Great Russell Street, London WC1B 3DG. Telephone: 071-636 1555.

Castle Museum, Norwich, Norfolk NR1 3JU. Telephone: 0603 222222 extension 71224.

Chichester District Museum, 29 Little London, Chichester, West Sussex PO19 1PB. Telephone: 0243 784683.

Museum of Sussex Archaeology, Barbican House, 169 High Street, Lewes, East Sussex BN7 1YE. Telephone: 0273 474379.

Worthing Museum and Art Gallery, Chapel Road, Worthing, West Sussex BN11 1HD. Telephone: 0903 39999 extension 121.

There is also a good display of neolithic flint mining and the Brandon gun-flint industry at:

Brandon Heritage Centre, George Street, Brandon, Suffolk. Telephone: 0842 811380.

9
Further reading

General reading

Burton, J. 'Quarrying in a Tribal Society', *World Archaeology*, 16 (1984), 234-47.

Burton, J. 'Exchange Pathways at a Stone Axe Factory in Papua New Guinea' in G. de G. Sieveking and M. H. Newcomer (editors), *The Human Uses of Flint and Chert*, 183-91. Cambridge University Press, 1987.

Clough, T. H. McK., and Cummins, W. A. *Stone Age Studies*. CBA Research Report 23, 1979.

Cummins, W. A. 'Stone Axes as a Guide to Neolithic Communications and Boundaries in England and Wales', *Proceedings of the Prehistoric Society*, 46 (1980), 45-60.

Curwen, E. C. *The Archaeology of Sussex*, Methuen, 1954.

Drewett, P., Rudling, D., and Gardiner, M. *The South East to AD 1000*. Longman, 1988.

Gardiner, J. P. 'Flint Procurement and Neolithic Axe Production on the South Downs: a Re-assessment', *Oxford Journal of Archaeology*, 9 (1990), 119-40.

Forrest, A. J. *Masters of Flint*. Terence Dalton, 1983.

Healy, F. 'Farming and Field Monuments: the Neolithic in Norfolk' in C. Barringer (editor), *Aspects of East Anglian Pre-history*, 77-140. Geo Books, 1984.

Pitts, M. *Later Stone Implements*. Shire, 1980.

Sieveking, G. de G. 'Grimes Graves and Prehistoric European Flint Mining' in H. Crawford (editor), *Subterranean Britain. Aspects of Underground Archaeology*, 1-43. John Baker, 1979.

Site reports

Curwen, E., and Curwen, E. C. 'Harrow Hill Flint Mine Excavation, 1924-5', *Sussex Archaeological Collections*, 67 (1926), 103-38.

Mercer, R. J. *Grimes Graves, Norfolk: Excavations 1971-72*. Department of the Environment Archaeological Reports Number 11, 1981.

Pull, J. H. *The Flint Miners of Blackpatch*. Williams and Norgate, 1932.

Pye, E. M. *The Flint Mines at Blackpatch, Church Hill and Cissbury, Sussex. A Report on the late J. H. Pull's Excavations 1922-1955*. Unpublished MA dissertation, University of Edinburgh, 1968.

Stone, J. F. S. 'Easton Down, Winterslow, S. Wilts., Flint Mine Excavation, 1930', *Wiltshire Archaeological and Natural History Magazine*, 45 (1932), 350-65.

Index

Page numbers in italic refer to illustrations.